FlyingKids Presents:
Kids' Travel Guide
Japan

Author: Damien Selby

Editor: Carma Graber

Graphic designer: Neboysha Dolovacki

Cover Illustrations and design: Francesca Guido

Published by FlyingKids Limited

Visit us @ www.theflyingkids.com

Contact us: leonardo@theflyingkids.com

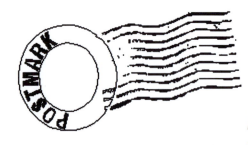

ISBN: 978-1-910994-56-6

Copyright © 2017 Shira Halperin and FlyingKids Limited

All rights reserved. No part of this publication may be reproduced, stored in retrieval systems, or transmitted by any means, including electronic, mechanical, photocopying, or otherwise, without prior written permission of the publisher and copyright holder.

Although the authors and FlyingKids have taken all reasonable care in preparing this book, we make no warranty about the accuracy or completeness of its content and, to the maximum extent permitted, disclaim all liability arising from its use.

Acknowledgments:

All images are Sutterstock.com or public domain.

Editorial credits (shutterstock.com): 14c- By jack_photo; 14b- By b-hide the scene; 16m-By Luciano Mortula – LGM; 16br-By HIROSHI H; 17t-By MrNovel; 17c-By Punyaphat Larpsomboon; 17b-By Vladimir Zhoga; 18c-By Cuson; 20c-By littlewormy; 25b-By weniliou; 27b-By Pumidol; 27bg-By Sarunyu L; 28t- By Denis Makarenko; 28c-By pio3; 28c- By isaac jose sanchez meza; 34b-By J. Henning Buchholz; 35m-By lit3rd; 36b- By hayachanta; 37b-By MAHATHIR MOHD YASIN.

Key: t=top; b=bottom; l=left; r=right; c=center; m=main image; bg=background

Table of Contents

Dear Parents	4
Hi, Kids!	5
A travel diary—the beginning!	6
Preparations at home—do not forget	8
Welcome to Japan!	10
Japan on the map—thousands of islands	11
What is a compass rose?	12
Japan's borders	13
Japan's busy capital: Tokyo	14
Magical Kyoto: an adventure in Japanese culture	15
Osaka: a modern side of Japan	16
Nara: the home of friendly deer	17
Hakone ... get away from the city	18
A tropical paradise	19
A winter world	20
The flags and symbols of Japan	21
What money do Japanese people use?	22
Japan's history	23
Meet the samurai and the geisha	25
Japanese folktales—an animal story for you to enjoy	26
Famous people in Japan	27
Japanese food—sushi, sweets, and more	29
Learn some Japanese words	32
Special things you'll see in Japan	34
Only in Japan	36
Fun facts about Japan	37
What do you know about Japan?	38
Games and activities	39
Summary of the trip	40
A journal	42
Enjoy more fun adventures with Leonardo	44

This is the only page for parents in this book ...

Dear Parents,

If you bought this book, you're probably planning a family trip with your kids. You are spending a lot of time and money in the hopes that this family vacation will be pleasant and fun. You would like your children to learn a little about the country you visit—its geography, history, unique culture, traditions, and more. And you hope they will always remember the trip as a very special experience.

The reality is often quite different. Parents find themselves frustrated as they struggle to convince their kids to join a tour or visit a landmark, while the kids just want to stay in and watch TV. On the road, the children are glued to their mobile devices instead of enjoying the new sights and scenery—or they complain and constantly ask, "When are we going to get there?" Many parents are disappointed after they return home and discover that their kids don't remember much about the trip and the new things they learned.

That's exactly why *Kids' Travel Guide — Japan* was created.

How does it work?

A family trip is fun. But difficulties can arise when children are not in their natural environment. *Kids' Travel Guide — Japan* takes this into account and supports children as they get ready for the trip, visit new places, learn new things, and finally, return home.

Kids' Travel Guide — Japan does this by helping children to prepare for the trip and know what to expect. During the trip, kids will read relevant facts about Japan and get advice on how to adapt to new situations. The kids will meet Leonardo—their tour guide. Leonardo encourages them to experiment, explore, and be more involved in the family's activities—as well as to learn new information and make memories throughout the trip.

Kids' Travel Guide — Japan includes puzzles, tasks to complete, useful tips, and other recommendations along the way. In addition, kids are asked to document and write about their experiences during the trip, so that when you return home, they will have a memoir that will be fun to look at and reread again and again.

Kids' Travel Guide — Japan offers general information about Japan, so it is useful regardless of the city or part of the country you plan to visit. It includes basic geography; flag, symbols, and coins; basic history; and colorful facts about culture and customs in Japan.

Ready for a new experience?
Have a nice trip and have fun!

Hi, Kids!

If you are reading this book, it means you are lucky—you are going to **Japan**!

You probably already know what areas you will visit, and you may have noticed that **your parents** are getting ready for the journey. They have bought **travel guides**, looked for information on the **Internet**, and **printed pages** of information. They are talking to friends and people who have already visited **Japan**, in order to learn about it and know what to do, where to go, and when … But this is not just another **guidebook** for your parents.

THIS BOOK IS FOR YOU ONLY—THE YOUNG TRAVELER.

So what is this book all about?

First and foremost, meet **Leonardo**, your very own personal guide on this trip. **Leonardo** has visited many places around the **world** (guess how he got there 😉), and he will be with you throughout the **book** and the **trip**. **Leonardo** will tell you all **about** the **places** you will visit—it is always good to learn a little bit about the country and its history beforehand. He will provide many **ideas**, **quizzes**, **tips**, and **other surprises**. **Leonardo** will accompany you while you are packing and leaving home. He will stay in the **hotel** with you (don't worry, it does not cost more money 😉)! And he will see the sights with you until you **return home**.

A Travel Diary – The Beginning!
Going to Japan!!!

How did you get to Japan?

By plane / ship / other _____

We will stay in Japan for _____ days.

Is this your first visit? yes / no

Where will you sleep? In a hotel / In a *ryokan* (inn) / In an apartment / With family / Other _____

What places are you planning to visit?

_____
_____
_____

What special activities are you planning to do?

_____
_____
_____

Are you excited about the trip?
This is an excitement indicator. Ask your family members how excited they are (from "not at all" up to "very, very much"), and mark each of their answers on the indicator. Leonardo has already marked the level of his excitement …

not at all   very, very much

Leonardo

Who is traveling?

Write down the names of the family members traveling with you and their answers to the questions.

Paste a picture of your family.

Name: _____

Age: _____

Have you visited Japan before? yes / no

What is the most exciting thing about your upcoming trip?

_____
_____

Name: _____

Age: _____

Have you visited Japan before? yes / no

What is the most exciting thing about your upcoming trip?

_____
_____

Name: _____

Age: _____

Have you visited Japan before? yes / no

What is the most exciting thing about your upcoming trip?

_____
_____

Name: _____

Age: _____

Have you visited Japan before? yes / no

What is the most exciting thing about your upcoming trip?

_____
_____

Name: _____

Age: _____

Have you visited Japan before? yes / no

What is the most exciting thing about your upcoming trip?

_____
_____

Preparations at home – DO NOT FORGET …!

Mom or Dad will take care of packing clothes (how many pairs of pants, which comb to take …). Leonardo will only tell you the stuff he thinks you might want to bring along on your trip to Japan.

Leonardo made a Packing List for you. Check off each item as you pack it!

- ☐ *Kids' Travel Guide — Japan* — of course 😉
- ☐ Comfortable walking shoes
- ☐ A raincoat or umbrella (Sometimes it rains without warning.)
- ☐ A hat (and sunglasses, if you want)
- ☐ Pens and pencils
- ☐ Crayons and markers (It is always nice to color and paint.)
- ☐ A notebook or writing pad (You can use it for games or writing, or to draw or doodle in when you're bored …)
- ☐ A book to read
- ☐ Your smartphone/tablet or camera

Pack your things in a small bag (or backpack).

You may also want to take these things:

Snacks, fruit, candy, and chewing gum. If you are flying, it can help a lot during **takeoff and landing**, when there's pressure in your ears.

Games you can play **while sitting down:** electronic games, booklets of crossword puzzles, connect-the-numbers (or connect-the-dots), etc.

Now let's see if you can find 12 items you should take on a trip in this word search puzzle:

- ☐ Leonardo
- ☐ walking shoes
- ☐ hat
- ☐ raincoat
- ☐ crayons
- ☐ book
- ☐ pencil
- ☐ camera
- ☐ snacks
- ☐ fruit
- ☐ patience
- ☐ good mood

P	A	T	I	E	N	C	E	A	W	F	G
E	L	R	T	S	G	Y	J	W	A	T	O
Q	E	Y	U	Y	K	Z	K	M	L	W	O
H	O	S	N	A	S	N	Y	S	K	G	N
A	N	R	Z	C	P	E	N	C	I	L	M
C	A	M	E	R	A	A	W	G	N	E	O
R	R	A	I	N	C	O	A	T	G	Q	O
Y	D	S	G	I	R	K	Z	K	S	H	D
S	O	A	C	O	A	E	T	K	H	A	T
F	R	U	I	T	Y	Q	O	V	O	D	A
B	O	O	K	F	O	H	Z	K	E	R	T
T	K	Z	K	A	N	S	I	E	S	Y	U
O	V	I	E	S	S	N	A	C	K	S	P

Welcome to Japan!

Nihon is the Japanese word for Japan. *Nihon* means **"the land of the rising sun."** More than 20 million people visit the country every year. There are so many interesting things to do and see in Japan. You'll have fun discovering the unusual sights, history, and customs. Get ready for an adventure!

Leonardo fell in love with Japan as soon as he got there. He hopes you will too. So in this book, he's going to share all the interesting things he knows about Japan! 🙂

One of Leonardo's favorite things about Japan is the mountains. More than **70 percent** of Japan is made up of **mountains and volcanoes**. Japan has 100 active volcanoes*—more than almost any country in the **world!**

*A **volcano** usually looks like a **mountain**. If we could travel **into** a volcano, we would find a **pool** of **melted rock**. When a **volcano erupts**, that hot liquid rock— called "lava"—can reach the surface!

Around **126 million** people live in Japan. That's a lot of people! The Japanese people are known for being **friendly**, and they usually **bow** when they meet someone. In Japan, bowing is a way of showing **respect**.

10

Japan on the map—
thousands of islands!

Japan is on the continent of **Asia**. The country is made up of more than **6,000** islands, but only **430** of the islands have people living on them. The islands are called the **Japanese archipelago** (that's the word for a big group of islands).

There are four main islands that make up Japan. Do you think you can help Leonardo find their names? _____, _____, _____, and _____.

Answers: Hokkaido, Honshu, Shikoku, and Kyushu.

Answer: Japan's four main islands are Hokkaido, Honshu, Shikoku, and Kyushu.

Did you know?
Every year there are around **1,500 earthquakes** in Japan. An earthquake is where the ground **shakes** under your feet. But don't worry—most of the earthquakes in Japan are **so small** that you can't feel them!

Can you see the country that is closest to Japan on the map? What's the name of the country? _____

Hint: It's near the bottom of the **Sea of Japan**!

What is a compass rose?

A compass rose is a design that shows the **directions**:
North – South – East – West. Since **North** is always marked on maps, you can always figure out where the other directions are.
A compass rose is drawn on the face of a compass, and the **hand always points North**. When you know where each direction is, it is easier to figure out where you are … and how to get to where you want to be.

Write down the three missing directions in the blank squares.

North

Japan is **surrounded** by water. There are no countries right next to it. Can you spot the ocean and different seas around Japan on the map?

To the West – _____ and _____ .
To the East – _____ .
To the North – _____ .

Answers:
West – Sea of Japan, East China Sea.
East – North Pacific Ocean.
North: Sea of Okhotsk.

Japan's borders

Did you know?
In order to separate **different** countries, borders were invented. A border is a line that marks the end of one country's **territory** and the beginning of another. There are all kinds of borders—sometimes a river or a range of mountains form a **natural** border, and sometimes a fence or special gate is built to mark a border.

The islands that make up Japan have no borders at all—do you know why? It's because Japan is completely **surrounded** by water.

There are **three** countries that are quite close to Japan, can you help Leonardo find them?

_____ , _____ , and _____ .

Answers: North Korea, South Korea, and Russia

Quizzes!

You are about to visit beautiful Japan. Can you find 10 Japanese cities in the word search puzzle?

- ☐ Tokyo
- ☐ Kyoto
- ☐ Yokohama
- ☐ Nagasaki
- ☐ Osaka
- ☐ Hiroshima
- ☐ Nagoya
- ☐ Sendai
- ☐ Sapporo
- ☐ Chiba

Y	H	P	P	E	I	F	X	K	S	H	F
A	B	I	H	C	U	G	A	B	I	B	K
C	O	F	A	N	M	O	K	R	T	J	Y
T	K	P	G	M	C	R	O	M	S	L	O
V	O	Z	I	K	A	S	A	G	A	N	T
Q	P	K	N	J	H	H	A	F	B	C	O
B	E	D	Y	I	D	Y	O	M	M	Z	R
Q	C	O	M	O	O	A	Y	K	A	I	O
I	M	A	S	G	L	F	J	G	O	Q	P
O	E	A	A	S	E	N	D	A	I	Y	P
W	K	N	A	Z	K	T	Q	L	C	P	A
A	U	H	D	B	U	K	P	R	I	Y	S

13

Japan's busy capital city: Tokyo!

The **capital** of Japan is called **Tokyo**, and it is one of the **busiest** cities in the world! This is because more than **13 million** people call Tokyo their **home**.

Tokyo was not always the capital of Japan. It became the capital when the **Emperor of Japan** moved to Tokyo from Kyoto all the way back in **1868!** His name was **Emperor Meiji**, and he was the emperor until **1912**.

If you really want to see all of Tokyo at once, you can go to the top of **Tokyo Skytree, the tallest tower** in the world. It's **634 meters** (or almost 2,100 feet) tall! Japan has a lot of **earthquakes**, so the tower had to be built to survive them.

Like a rocket!
One of Leonardo's **favorite** things to do in Tokyo is to **ride** on the *Shinkansen*, or **bullet train**. From Tokyo, you can catch a bullet train to lots of different Japanese cities! It goes really fast—**321** kilometers per hour (or about 200 miles per hour)! That's almost **three** times faster than a **cheetah**! 😲

What's **your** favorite way to travel?

Ancient Buddhist temple
One of the most **famous** buildings in Tokyo is an **ancient Buddhist temple** called **Senso-ji**. It was built more than **1,000 years ago**! Over **30 million** people visit it every single year!

Did you know?
In Tokyo there are lots of **activities** for you to do with your family. You can even go to **Disneyland**. It was the first one to be built outside of America!

Magical Kyoto: an adventure in Japanese culture

Kyoto is one of the most **cultural** cities in the world, and it's a lot more calm and laid-back than busy Tokyo.

Kyoto is known as the **"thousand-year capital."** That's because it was the emperor's home for more than a thousand years before he moved to Tokyo.

There are a lot of fun things to do in **Kyoto**—and Leonardo loves trying to do them all! 😉 Here are some of Leonardo's favorite things to see:

Fushimi Inari-Taisha: One of the most famous shrines (holy places) in the world.

Kinkaku-ji: A temple famous for looking like gold.

Kyoto Tower: A tower you can go up in to see the whole city and the forests that surround it!

Festival time!
The *Gion Matsuri* is one of the most famous **festivals** in Japan. It has been happening for more than a **thousand** years! It takes place during the entire month of July, and it has a lot of different events.

One of the best events is the **parade** of floats. You can even see them being built just before the festival! Years ago the Japanese people would pick a young boy to carry messages to the **spirits** during the parade—and they still do this today!

 Can you guess which of these buildings is **Kinkaku-ji**?

Did you know?
Kyoto has its own **bamboo forest** called *Arashiyama*. The bamboo trees are even taller than houses! There is a **monkey park** near the bamboo forest, and people can feed the monkeys **bananas**, **apples**, and **peanuts**! 😉

Osaka: a modern side of Japan

Osaka is the **third largest** city in Japan. Ten and a-half million people live there. It is one of the main cities for **business**. Lots of Japan's shipping happens in the **ship docks** at Osaka.

During **World War II**, Osaka lost most of its **historical** buildings. That means Osaka now looks like a very **modern** city—similar to American cities.

Puppet Theater!
A very special type of **theater** was created in Osaka way back in 1805. It is called *bunraku*, but we would call it a "**puppet theater**." Each puppet is made with lots of small **details**. In fact, there are so many details that it takes three **puppeteers** (people who control puppets) to control just one single puppet! Leonardo likes watching the puppets dance!

Can you connect both of these famous buildings to their descriptions below?

A The **Umeda Sky** Building has **two** really **tall** towers that connect right at the top!

B **Osaka castle** has a **green roof** that's **decorated** with lots of **gold animals**!

Did you know?
The first Universal Studios built outside of America is in Osaka! 🙂 It is full of different **Harry Potter** attractions, and children can even ride a pretend **Hippogriff**. It also has Snoopy, Hello Kitty, Sesame Street, and Spider-Man.

Aswers: A=2; B=1

16

Nara: the home of friendly deer

Kyoto is the **cultural** capital of Japan. But Nara is even **older** than Kyoto! It was the **capital** of Japan even before Kyoto— back in the year 710. That's more than a thousand years ago!

Did you know?
There are eight *UNESCO World Heritage sites in Nara.

*A **UNESCO World Heritage** site is a place that is considered so outstanding and important that it gets special protection.

One of the most **famous** temples in all of Japan can be found in **Nara**. It is called **Todaiji**, which means **"Great Eastern Temple."** It was built long ago, and it is the **head temple** of all the **Buddhist temples** in Japan.

But Nara Park is **famous** for another reason— deer! It is the home to more than **1,200** deer, and you can even feed the deer by hand!

Can you guess what the deer like to eat? Clue: Leonardo likes them too!

Answer: Crackers!

Did you know?
The Japanese **word** for **deer** is **shika**. Leonardo can help you say it: **shee-kah**.

You can find the **largest bronze** Buddha in the world inside of Todaiji! He was built more than a **thousand** years ago, when Nara was still the **capital** of Japan. He is almost **22 meters** (or 72 feet) **tall**.

Hakone ... Get away from the city!

Hakone is one of the **top** tourist destinations in Japan! In fact, Hakone makes almost all its **money** from **tourism**. Leonardo likes being a **tourist**! Do you? 😉

People like **Hakone** because it's in the country—but it's also really **close** to Tokyo.

There are a lot of fun things to see in Hakone. There is even a **volcanic** valley, and you can still see gas and steam coming out of it! It is called **Owakudani**. At Owakudani, you can eat *kura-tamago*, which means "**black** egg"! (The way the eggs are cooked turns them black.)

High in the sky!
Getting to Owakudani is **fun** too! You get to take a ride on the **Hakone Ropeway**, which is a cable car—like the ones people use when they go **skiing**. From **high** up in the air, you can see all around Hakone!

Let's pretend!
Leonardo likes to **pretend** to be a **pirate** when he is in Hakone. 😜 This is because **pirate ships** travel across **Lake Ashi** every day—and you can go on them!

Did you know?
Next to Lake Ashi, there is a volcano called **Mount Hakone**. It last erupted about 2,900 years ago. That's a long, long time!

A tropical paradise—
Okinawa

One area of Japan is **very warm**, no matter what time of year it is. That's because it's **tropical**, like Hawaii!

It's called **Okinawa**, and it's a large island. In fact, it's the largest in the island chain south of **Kyushu**. (Do you remember? Kyushu is one of Japan's four main islands.)

Okinawa was **not** always a part of Japan. It became a part of Japan in **1609**, when it was invaded by people from Japan!

Sea animals!
The **warm climate** means that the **sea animals** in Okinawa are very special. There are lots of **sea turtles** and **jellyfish**! That's why many people like **scuba diving** around the island.

Leonardo is a bit too **small** to go scuba diving … Instead, he likes going to the **Okinawa Churaumi Aquarium**. The biggest whale shark in the world lives there. It's 12 meters (40 feet) long.

Can you help Leonardo spot the whale shark? 😉

Did you know?
A very **special** type of cat lives in Okinawa. It cannot be found anywhere else in the world! It is called an **Iriomote cat**. The Iriomote cat is **endangered**, which means there aren't many left in the world.

A winter world— Hokkaido

Hokkaido is one of Japan's **four main** islands! The name Hokkaido means **"Northern Sea Route."**

Hokkaido is the **opposite** of Okinawa , and it is almost always cold there. This is because Hokkaido is in the **northernmost** part of Japan. It's very close to Russia **on the map**. The Japanese people that live on Hokkaido have learned how to live with the **snow** and **ice**.

Dogsled racing!

Dogsled racing is a sport that is famous in Alaska, and across Scandinavia. In the **1980s**, a **famous Japanese adventurer** called Uemura Naomi brought Eskimo dogs back to Japan from Alaska. They were given as a gift to one of the **main** cities of Hokkaido. And that's when dogsled racing **started** in Japan!

Did you know?
In **Hokkaido**, children have their own **dogsled contests**!

The capital of Hokkaido is called **Sapporo**, and every year Sapporo has a **Snow Festival**! During the **Snow Festival** people build their own **ice sculptures** and **snow sculptures**. They make **historic buildings**, **people**, and even **animals** out of ice and snow!

If you were going to a **snow festival,** what kind of **sculpture** would you **create**?

Did you know?
One of the **cutest** animals in Japan lives in Hokkaido! It's called an *ezo momonga*, or **flying** **squirrel**.

The flags and symbols of Japan!

This is the **flag of Japan**!

It's a **white** flag with a **red** circle in the middle.

The flag is called *nisshoki*, which means "sun-mark flag." But most Japanese people call it *hinomaru*, which means "circle of the sun" or "rising sun."

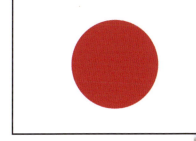

No one really knows where the **design** for this flag came from. Most people agree that it was created to represent Japan's nickname, "Land of the Rising Sun."

It was first used back in **701**, by Emperor Mommu. But Japan didn't make it the official flag until **1999**!

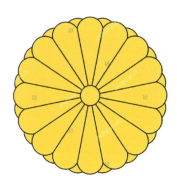

This is the **Imperial Seal of Japan**. It is also called the **Chrysanthemum Seal**, but Leonardo needs help saying that word!

It's the **national seal** of Japan, and it can only be used by the **Emperor of Japan**!

Japanese people believe that Koi fish or images of Koi fish will bring them good fortune and good luck. Can you draw a picture of a Koi fish?

Do you have a symbol or an object that you believe will bring you good luck?

What money do Japanese people use?

In Japan, people use a type of money that is called **Japanese yen!** The sign for Japanese yen is ¥.

Japanese coins

Coins are not worth very much in Japan. But there are six **different** Japanese coins that you can see.

Can you draw the sign for Leonardo?

Did you know?
It costs ¥3 to make a ¥1 coin!

1-yen coin   5-yen coin   10-yen coin

50-yen coin   100-yen coin   500-yen coin

In Japan, you're likely to see people paying for things with **bank notes**, not **coins**. The most common notes are ¥1000, ¥2000, ¥5000, and ¥10,000. That **might** seem like a lot of **money**, but ¥1000 is actually **less** then $10!

Leonardo needs your **help**! Can you help him figure out which bank note is which? **Connect** each bank note to the right amount below.

○ ¥5000   ○ ¥10,000   ○ ¥1000   ○ ¥2000

Japan's history: beginning in ancient times

The **history** of Japan is **interesting**, because it is full of lots of **different** **people** and **cultures**.

Follow Leonardo on a **journey** through **Japanese history** …

Around **30,000 years ago**, the first **people** traveled to Japan. They got to Japan by **crossing land bridges** between **Siberia** and Japan—and between **South Korea** and Japan. Those land bridges have now been **covered** by the sea! 😲

Thousands of years after people first came to Japan, the **first official** Japanese **society** appeared. That society is now known as **Jomon culture**. It appeared around **12,000 years ago**—at the same time that the **Ainu** people began to arrive by **boat**! They came to Japan from Siberia.

The **Jomon** and **Ainu** people **survived** for thousands of years. They **hunted**, **fished**, and **gathered fruit** and **vegetables**. Today, we can still see all the **tools** that they used! They had **homemade stone tools** like **knives** and **axes**. They also used to **weave** baskets to carry objects and food in.

It would take **thousands** more years for **Japanese society** to have an **emperor**. The first **Emperor of Japan** came to power around **2,600 years ago**! His name was **Jimmu Tenno**.

Quizzes!

How did the first people **travel** to Japan? _____

What was the name of Japan's first **emperor**? _____

Answers:
1. Over land bridges
2. Jimmu Tenno

Japan's history: from long ago to today ...

2,300 years ago: The **Yayoi people** came to **Honshu** from both **South Korea** and **China**.

The **Yayoi people** were very good at **growing** rice in rice paddies (flooded fields). That's when the **rice industry** that would **feed** Japan began.

900 years ago: The **emperor** lost control of **power** in Japan. Instead, **military** people called **shoguns** took over.

About 500 years ago: The first **Europeans** arrived in Japan. They brought **weapons** and **Christianity** with them. Christianity was different from any religion that already **existed** in Japan.

About 400 years ago: The **shogun** who had gained power in Japan **outlawed** all travel. This means that Japanese people **could not** visit the rest of the world, and no one could visit Japan.

200 years ago: Treaties were signed so that people from Japan could once again **travel the world.** At around the same time, the **emperor** regained power, and Japan was much more **peaceful**.

Quizzes!

Leonardo is finding all this information a bit confusing! Can you help him remember it correctly? Mark True or False.

1. The **Yayoi people** were very good at growing wheat. True / False

2. 1,000 years ago: The first **Europeans** arrived in Japan. True / False

3. 400 years ago: The **shogun encouraged all Japanese to travel around the world.** True / False

4. 200 years ago: Japan became much more **peaceful**. True / False

Answers: 1. False; 2. False; 3. False; 4. True

Meet the samurai!

Samurai were Japanese **warriors** who came from **noble** and **important families**. They were masters of **martial arts**, and they were very **respected** by the Japanese people.

Lords (people who owned **land**) would **employ** samurai to protect their land. In **ancient Japan**, they did not pay the samurai with **money**—instead they paid them with **rice**!

Did you know?
More than a **thousand** years ago, some women also trained to be samurai. They learned lots of **martial arts** and **strategy**!

Samurai could carry **two swords**—a long sword called a *katana*, and a short sword called a *tanto*.

Meet the geisha!

A **geisha** is a Japanese woman who works as an **entertainer**. In Japanese, the word *geisha* means "**artist**." Geisha were really common around **200 years ago**, but now only a small number of geisha are left in **Japan**.

Japanese people call the **world** that geisha are a part of *karyukai*. It means "the **flower** and **willow** world." This is because geisha are **beautiful** like flowers, but **strong** like trees.

Did you know?
If you see a **geisha** in **white** make-up, wearing a **colorful** kimono, what you are actually seeing is a *maiko* (a young woman in training to be a geisha). Geisha only wear white make-up during **special events**!

Japanese Folktales—
an animal story for you to enjoy

Nezumi no Yomeiri (The Mouse's Marriage)

A long time ago in Japan, there lived a **wealthy** mouse family. The Father Mouse and Mother Mouse were really **proud** of their daughter, so they wanted her to **marry** someone special.

Father Mouse thought that **Mr. Sun** was the most important person in the world, because he **lit** it up! But when they went to see Mr. Sun, he told them about **Mr. Cloud**, who could easily **cover** him up!

When they went to see **Mr. Cloud**, he told them about **Mr. Wind**, who could easily **blow** him away! When they went to see Mr. Wind, he told them about **Mr. Wall**, who could **stop** his wind instantly!

Something **special** happened when they went to see **Mr. Wall**. Mr. Wall showed them that his wall was **covered in holes**, and who made those holes? **Mice**! So the daughter of Father and Mother Mouse could marry another mouse—and live happily ever after!

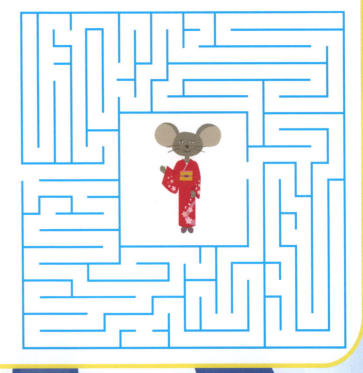

Help Mr. and Mrs. Mouse get to their daughter mouse.

Famous people in Japan: meet Toyotomi Hideyoshi and Emperor Akihito!

Toyotomi Hideyoshi

Toyotomi Hideyoshi was one of the most powerful lords in Japan. He was also a **general**, a **samurai**, and even a **politician**. He lived **around 500** years ago. He **united** Japan and made it a **safe** place.

He also found the **money** to **build** and repair some of Japan's most famous temples. You can **still** see a lot of them today. Most are in **Kyoto**.

While he was a **general**, the ruler of Japan, Nobunaga, passed away. So Toyotomi Hideyoshi became the ruler of Japan! The **Emperor of Japan** was still the official ruler, but Toyotomi made sure that everyday life in Japan was **nice** and **safe**.

Emperor Akihito

Emperor Akihito is the **current** Emperor of Japan. He is **descended** from the first-ever Emperor of Japan—which means his family has ruled for **thousands** of years. He grew up during **World War II**. Because of that, he believes in **peace and unity**. 🙂

He was 55 years old when he became emperor. Japanese people call his reign the **Heisei Period**, which means "**achieving peace**." In his **spare time**, Emperor Akihito likes to study fish. He especially enjoys studying a type of fish called gobies!

Who is your **favorite famous person?** _____
What is that person **famous** for? _____

Japanese Anime and Hayao Miyazaki!

Leonardo loves cartoon **movies**. Do you have a favorite cartoon? _____

One of Leonardo's **favorite Japanese people** is **Hayao Miyazaki**. Hayao is a **film director**, a **screenwriter**, an **author**, and most importantly—an **animator**!

He cofounded a **company** called **Studio Ghibli** in **Tokyo**. It is similar to **Disney** and **DreamWorks**, which means they create a lot of **cartoon movies** for **children**! Hayao uses Japanese **myths** and **folktales** to create characters.

What is anime?

Anime is the word for a **special** type of **Japanese animation**. But in Japan, people use the word "anime" to describe animation from all over the world. (Animation is what makes cartoons move and seem lifelike.)

Japanese anime is created for **all ages** to enjoy, so grown-ups can watch it too! The **characters** in Japanese animation look **unique**, and they usually have **very big eyes**.

Anime characters are usually **drawn by hand**, rather than using **computers**. This means that drawing the characters can take a **long time**!

It can be **difficult** for animators to draw different **emotions**. Can you try to make Leonardo look **happy**? How about sad? Give him a bored face too!

Happy Sad Bored

Bon appétit!
Japanese food—rice and fish make sushi!

Throughout their history, Japanese people have always eaten a lot of rice. Rice is grown by farmers in a flat field that is filled with water (called a "paddy"). Before they can harvest the rice, they have to drain all the water out of the field.

Almost every traditional Japanese meal involves rice—including breakfast! But rice can be eaten in a lot of different ways. It can be used to make crunchy rice crackers. Or it can be used to make sushi. It can even be used to make tasty cakes!

Sushi

Sushi!

Sushi is a type of traditional Japanese food. It is made of either raw(!) or cooked fish, and sometimes vegetables.

Sometimes sushi chefs will wrap sushi in a piece of seaweed that Japanese people call nori. It takes a whole 10 years of training before sushi chefs are allowed to serve food in restaurants!

Noodles!

Another important food in Japan is noodles. There are many different kinds of noodles—but the two main types are *ramen* noodles and *udon* noodles. Ramen noodles are very thin, and udon noodles are very thick. Leonardo likes eating noodles in Japan because he is allowed to slurp! In Japan, slurping shows the chef that you think the noodles are delicious! 🙂

Ramen noodles

What Japanese food did you like best? _____

What food did you not like? _____

Bon appétit! A different kind of sweet!

Traditional Japanese sweets are called *wagashi*. They are very different from the sweets in other countries!

There are lots of different types of *wagashi*—and they change with the seasons of the year. In the colder months, Japanese people eat *oshiruko*, which is a type of sweet soup. In warmer weather, Japanese people eat *namagashi*. These are small cakes made in the shapes of nature—including flowers!

Two of the main types of *wagashi* are *taiyaki* and *dango*.

What are your favorite sweets?

Taiyaki

Taiyaki is a pancake that is shaped like a fish! It is always filled with some sort of paste. Traditionally, this is a red bean paste, but you can also find custard, chocolate, cheese, and even sweet potato!

Dango is a type of Japanese sweet that is made from rice flour. It is always served on a wooden stick! Usually it is coated with either red bean paste, green tea, or syrup.

Do you like Kit-Kat bars? They're very popular in Japan, where they come in many flavors—even banana!

Dango

Bon appétit!
Breakfast and table manners!

What do you eat for breakfast? _____

A **traditional Japanese breakfast** will commonly include:
- A bowl of **tasty** rice.
- Natto, which is made out of **soy beans**. Some people love it, and other people hate it!
- Miso soup.
- Chicken or fish!

This means that **breakfast** in Japan is almost like eating **dinner**! 😊

Dinner in Japan

Breakfast in Japan

Table manners in Japan are much like table manners in other countries. **Never** chew with your mouth open—and don't put too much in your mouth at once!

But what can you do when eating noodles that would be rude in other countries? (Hint: It lets the chef know you think the noodles taste good! 😉 See page 29.)

School lunch in **Japan** is a lot like **breakfast**! A Japanese school **lunch** is called *kyuushoku*.

Did you know?
One **special** thing about Japan is the **character cafes**. You can find cafes that are all about **cartoon characters**! 😉

How do you order food in Japanese?

Ordering food in Japan is very **easy**, but you will need to know a **little** bit of Japanese! Don't worry, a lot of Japanese cafés and restaurants have an **English menu**! 😉

Say PLEASE or kudasai

One of the most **important** words to use when you order food is *kudasai* (koo-da-si), which means "please." In **Japanese**, you say the name of the food you want to order, and then say **kudasai**!

Before eating in Japan

It is **polite** to say *itadakimasu* (it-a-da-kee-mas). It is a way of saying **thank you** for a lovely meal!

Want to order water?

Mizu means "water." So to order water, you would say *mizu, kudasai*.

Fish	Sakana	sah-kah-nah
Vegetables	Yasai	yah-sa-e
Egg	Tamago	tah-mah-goh
Sushi	Sushi	su-shi
Chicken	Toriniku	to-ri-ni-ku
Shrimp	Ebi	eh-bee
Fried Pork	Tonkatsu	ton-ka-tsu
Soup	Suupu	suu-pu
Hamburger	Hanbaagaa	han-bah-gah
Chips	Chippusu	chip-su
Jelly	Zerii	ze-ree

If you want to order **chips in Japanese** then you have to say:

Chipuu wo hitotsu onegai shimasu?

The food goes first! If you wanted to order **two plates** of chips then you would have to say:

Chipuu wo futatsu onegai shimasu?

Learn Japanese with us!

The Japanese language can be **difficult** to read, but it's very easy to **speak** Japanese. Leonardo wants to help you learn some important words you can use on your trip to Japan:

Do you speak English?	Eigo o hanasemasu ka?
Yes / No	Hai / iie
Please	Kudasai
Thank you	Arigato
Excuse me!	Sumimasen!
Where is the toilet?	Toire wa doku desu ka?
Good / Bad	Yoi / Warui
What is your name?	O-namae wa nan desu ka?
My name is Leonardo!	Watashi no namae wa Leonardo desu!
Good morning	ohayoo (o-ha-yoo)
Good afternoon	konnichiwa (koh-ne-chi-wah)
Good evening	konbanwa (kon-ban-wah)

Learn Japanese numbers!

1	Ichi	一
2	Ni	二
3	San	三
4	Yon	四
5	Go	五
6	Roku	六
7	Nana	七
8	Hachi	八
9	Kyuu	九
10	Juu	十

Angel

Way

Did you know?
The Japanese alphabet uses characters instead of letters. Here are the characters for some common words. Try to copy your favorite.

Love

Write your age in Japanese words: _____

Can you draw the Japanese symbol for your age? _____

Tiger

Flower

Dragon

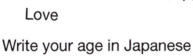
Spirit

Special things you'll see in Japan

Japanese Gardens

Japanese gardens are very special. There are **two** kinds of gardens. In history, **one** kind was owned by **emperors** and **noble families** who wanted a pretty garden! The other kind of **garden** gave **Buddhists** a **peaceful place** to **meditate**.

Buddhist Japanese gardens are usually called **Zen gardens**. They have a lot of **white sand** and **rocks**!

Japanese kimono

In Japan, you will see many **people** dressed in the **traditional clothing** called a *kimono*. **Men**, **women**, and **children** can all wear kimonos! Most men wear a *yukata*, which is made of **cotton fabric**. Kimonos are usually made of **silk**.

There are different **kinds** of kimonos. Two of the most **common** kinds are called *furisode* and *houmongi*. The *furisode* has **long, swinging sleeves**. It's worn by **women** who are not married. The *houmongi* is more formal. It's **only worn** by married women.

Sumo wrestling

The **national sport** of Japan is **sumo wrestling**! During a **sumo competition**, **one** sumo wrestler tries to get the **other** sumo wrestler out of the **ring** and onto the floor. Sumo wrestlers try to get as big as possible because more weight gives them an advantage. There are **six sumo tournaments** in Japan every year, and **tickets** for them **sell quickly**!

More things to see and do in Japan ...

Pink trees!

During the **spring**, Japanese people participate in *hanami*. *Hanami* means "flower viewing." It happens when the *sakura* appear on the trees. *Sakura* are **cherry blossoms**, and they make all of the trees look **pink**!

Pet bugs?!

A lot of children in Japan keep **beetles** as **pets**! 😲 The main type of beetle is called a *kabutomushi beetle* or **rhinoceros beetle**! They don't get as **big** as real rhinos do— but they can grow up to **3 inches** long!

If you could have any type of pet, what would it be? _____

A Japanese game ...

Leonardo wants you to try playing **janken**! Don't worry, it's not hard! Janken is the **Japanese** "rock, paper, scissors." But in Japan, there are **several ways** to play— including using your legs!

Instead of saying "rock, paper, scissors," you say *janken-pon*!

Try to play **janken** with your family! Write the winner's name here!

_____

The Japanese words for rock, paper, and scissors are:

 Rock: *Guu*

 Paper: *Paa*

 Scissors: *Choki*

Only in Japan

Nap time!
In Japan, men can **sleep** while they are at work! 🙂 They work for **long hours**, so taking **naps** lets their bosses know that they are working extra hard!

Adopt a grown man?!
In Japan, it is common for fully grown **men** to be **adopted**! This is because people want to pass down their **family businesses**. If they don't have a son to pass the business down to, then they just **adopt** one!

Did you know?
There are two different types of toilets that you can see in Japan. A **traditional** Japanese toilet is just a **hole** in the floor! But **modern** Japanese toilets have lots of different features and **buttons**! 🙂

Finding animals in the city
Japan has a lot of **animal cafés**. You can go into an animal café and meet **cats**, **hedgehogs**, and even **owls**! The people in the cafés will let you hold the animals. But Leonardo gets scared of the animals in the **reptile** cafés. Are you scared of snakes? Yes _____ No _____

Only big ones! _____

Japanese people live in **harmony** with nature. That means they look after the **natural features** around them. This is because many Japanese still follow the ancient **Shinto** religion.

Shinto teaches that everything in nature has its own spirit—including **mountains**, **waterfalls**, **forests**, and even **rocks**! These spirits are called *kami*.

Fun facts about Japan

The tallest mountain in Japan is called **Mount Fuji**. It is 3,776 meters (or almost two and a half miles) tall. That's the same as almost **3,000 gorillas** standing on top of each other!

The **busiest train station** in the world is Shinjuku Station in Tokyo. More than three million people use it every day!

Did you know?
The first man to travel to the **North Pole** on his own was Japanese! His name was **Naomi Uemura**, and he was an adventurer. But he went **missing** when he tried to climb Alaska's **Mount Denali** by himself in the **winter**.

The future!
Fortune cookies started in Japan. They have been **traced** all the way back to **Kyoto** in the 1800s.

Can you help Leonardo find all the words in the word search puzzle?

- ☐ Skytree
- ☐ Sumo
- ☐ Fortune cookie
- ☐ Sushi
- ☐ Janken
- ☐ Kabutomushi
- ☐ Sakura
- ☐ Sakana
- ☐ Kimono
- ☐ Yukata

S	A	D	S	C	C	A	O	S	Y
K	K	U	R	O	F	N	C	U	Y
A	M	Y	O	B	O	A	F	S	B
O	R	K	T	M	W	K	O	H	C
N	I	U	I	R	L	A	R	I	O
E	P	K	K	O	E	S	T	S	W
N	E	K	N	A	J	E	U	P	A
D	M	H	K	Z	S	C	N	C	L
Y	U	K	A	T	A	Y	E	K	B
Y	I	T	Q	V	F	S	H	N	D

What do you know about Japan?

1. What do Japanese people call Japan? _____

2. What are the names of the four main Japanese islands? _____

3. Can you name one of the closest countries to Japan? _____

4. What color is the national seal of Japan? _____

5. What type of money do they use in Japan? _____

6. Who was the samurai who ruled Japan? _____

7. How do you say "excuse me" in Japanese? _____

8. What food do Japanese people eat a lot of? _____

9. Who is the current ruler of Japan? _____

10. What pets do Japanese children love? _____

11. What was your favorite part of Japan? _____

Answers: 1. Nihon; 2. Honshu, Hokkaido, Shikoku, Kyushu; 3. South Korea, North Korea, Russia; 4. Yellow; 5. Yen; 6. Toyotomi Hideyoshi; 7. Sumimasen; 8. Rice; 9. Emperor Akihito; 10. Beetles.

Activities and games!

Try to unscramble these special Japanese words and places:

1. caVolno _____
2. Mntuo jFui _____
3. Zne raGned _____
4. tooKy _____
5. dasiaKu _____
6. hddButsi _____
7. moSu ginlWesrt _____

Answers: 1. Volcano; 2. Mount Fuji; 3. Zen Garden; 4. Kyoto; 5. Kudasai (please); 6. Buddhist; 7. Sumo Wrestling

Help Leonardo color the Japanese people in their traditional kimonos.

And to sum it all up ...

SUMMARY OF THE TRIP

We had great fun! What a pity it is over ...

Which places did we visit?

_____

_____

Whom did we meet ...
- Did you meet tourists from other countries? yes / no
  If you did meet tourists, where did they come from?
  (Name their nationalities):

_____

Shopping and souvenirs ...
- What did you buy on the trip?

_____

_____

- What did you want to buy, but ended up not buying?

_____

Experiences ...
- What are the most memorable experiences of the trip?

_____

_____

What was each family member's favorite place?

_____ : _____

_____ : _____

_____ : _____

_____ : _____

Grade the most **beautiful** places and the best **experiences** of your **journey**:

First place

Second place

Third place

And now, a difficult task—talk with your family and decide:

What did everyone enjoy most on the trip?

Date   What did we do?

A journal

Date · What did we do?

ENJOY MORE FUN ADVENTURES WITH LEONARDO AND FlyingKids

ITALY

THAILAND

JAPAN

FRANCE

GERMANY

SPAIN

AUSTRALIA

CHINA

USA

SPECIAL EDITIONS

UNITED KINGDOM

FOR FREE DOWNLOADS OF MORE ACTIVITIES, GO TO
WWW.THEFLYINGKIDS.COM

Printed in Germany
by Amazon Distribution
GmbH, Leipzig